I0813327

U.S. NATIONAL PARKS
HAWAI'I VOLCANOES
National Park
BY SARA GREEN
BLASTOFF! DISCOVERY
BLASTOFF! DISCOVERY, AN IMPRINT OF BELLWETHER MEDIA BY FLUTTERBEE

Blastoff! Discovery launches a new mission: reading to learn. Filled with facts and features, each book offers you an exciting new world to explore!

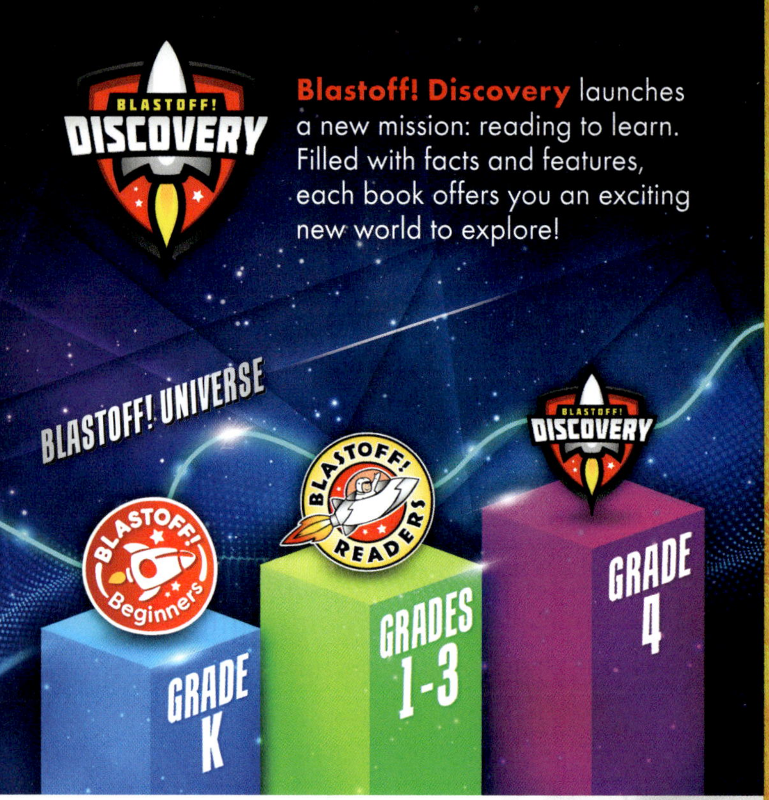

This edition first published in 2026 by Bellwether Media, Inc.

For information regarding permission, write to Bellwether Media, Inc., Attention: Permissions Department, 3500 American Blvd W, Suite 150, Bloomington, MN 55431.

Library of Congress Cataloging-in-Publication Data is available at www.loc.gov or upon request from the publisher.

ISBN: 9798893048490 (hardcover)
ISBN: 9798893049497 (ebook)

Editor: Elizabeth Neuenfeldt   Designer: Laura Sowers

Printed in the United States of America, North Mankato, MN.

TABLE OF CONTENTS

A VOLCANOES VACATION

A family arrives at Hawai'i **Volcanoes** National Park. They are excited to see a real volcano! They watch steam rising in the distance. It comes from Kīlauea, the most active volcano on Earth! The family hikes through a rainforest to Nāhuku. It is also called the Thurston **Lava Tube**. A river of lava made it around 500 years ago!

Next, the family visits Ha'akulamanu. It is also called the Sulfur Banks. Volcanic gases seep from the ground. They smell like rotten eggs! Then, the family drives the Chain of **Craters** Road. They see craters, lava, and ancient rock carvings. This park is incredible!

HAWAI'I VOLCANOES NATIONAL PARK

Hawai'i Volcanoes National Park is on the southeastern end of the island of Hawai'i, or the Big Island. This island is part of the state of Hawai'i. The park covers nearly 554 square miles (1,435 square kilometers). The land is **sacred** to **traditional** Hawaiian **culture**. It is home to Pele, the goddess of volcanoes.

Hawai'i Volcanoes has two active volcanoes, Kīlauea and Mauna Loa. Mauna Loa is the tallest. It rises 13,681 feet (4,170 meters) above **sea level**. The Kahuku Unit sits on the slopes of Mauna Loa. This hilly hiking area was once a large cattle ranch!

LONG MOUNTAIN
Mauna Loa means "long mountain" in Hawaiian. Mauna Loa is 75 miles (121 kilometers) long and 64 miles (103 kilometers) wide.
MAUNA LOA

THE LAND

LAVA LAND

Kīlauea has been erupting since 1983. As its lava flows and cools, new land is added to the Big Island.

The Hawaiian Islands formed millions of years ago. A **hot spot** deep within Earth pushed **magma** up to the floor of the Pacific Ocean. Lava came out and cooled. As it continued to **erupt**, layers of lava piled up to form a volcano.

Meanwhile, Earth's upper layer slowly moved across the hot spot. It carried the volcano off the hot spot, making it **dormant**. Then, a new volcano began to form above the hot spot. This process made the Hawaiian Islands. It continues today. Kīlauea and Mauna Loa are inside the park and are currently over the hot spot. They both remain active!

HOW THE HAWAIIAN ISLANDS FORMED

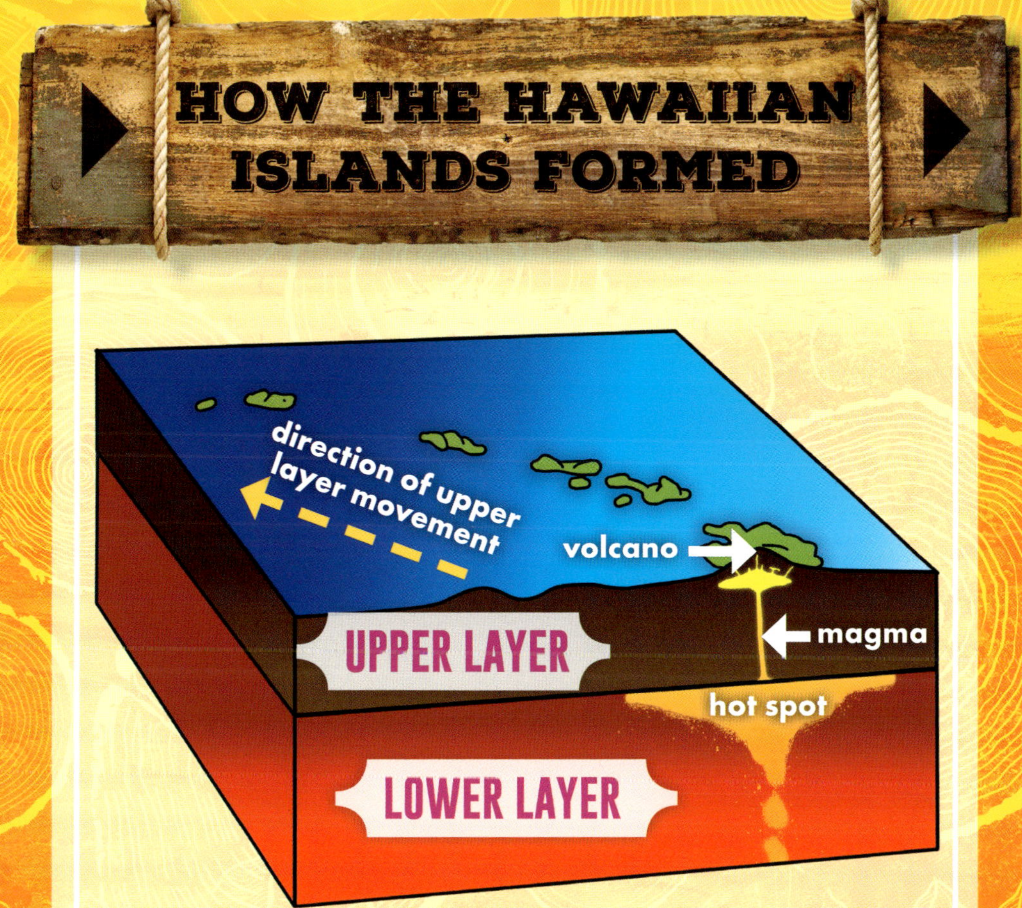

Volcanic activity made many of the park's features. Lava fields form when hot lava cools. Craters are made when the ground collapses. Volcanic ash made the **dunes** that spread across the Ka'ū Desert. Rainforests grow on the slopes of the volcanoes.

TYPES OF LAVA

Two kinds of lava are found in the park. 'A'ā lava is rough and jagged. Pāhoehoe lava is smooth and ropy.

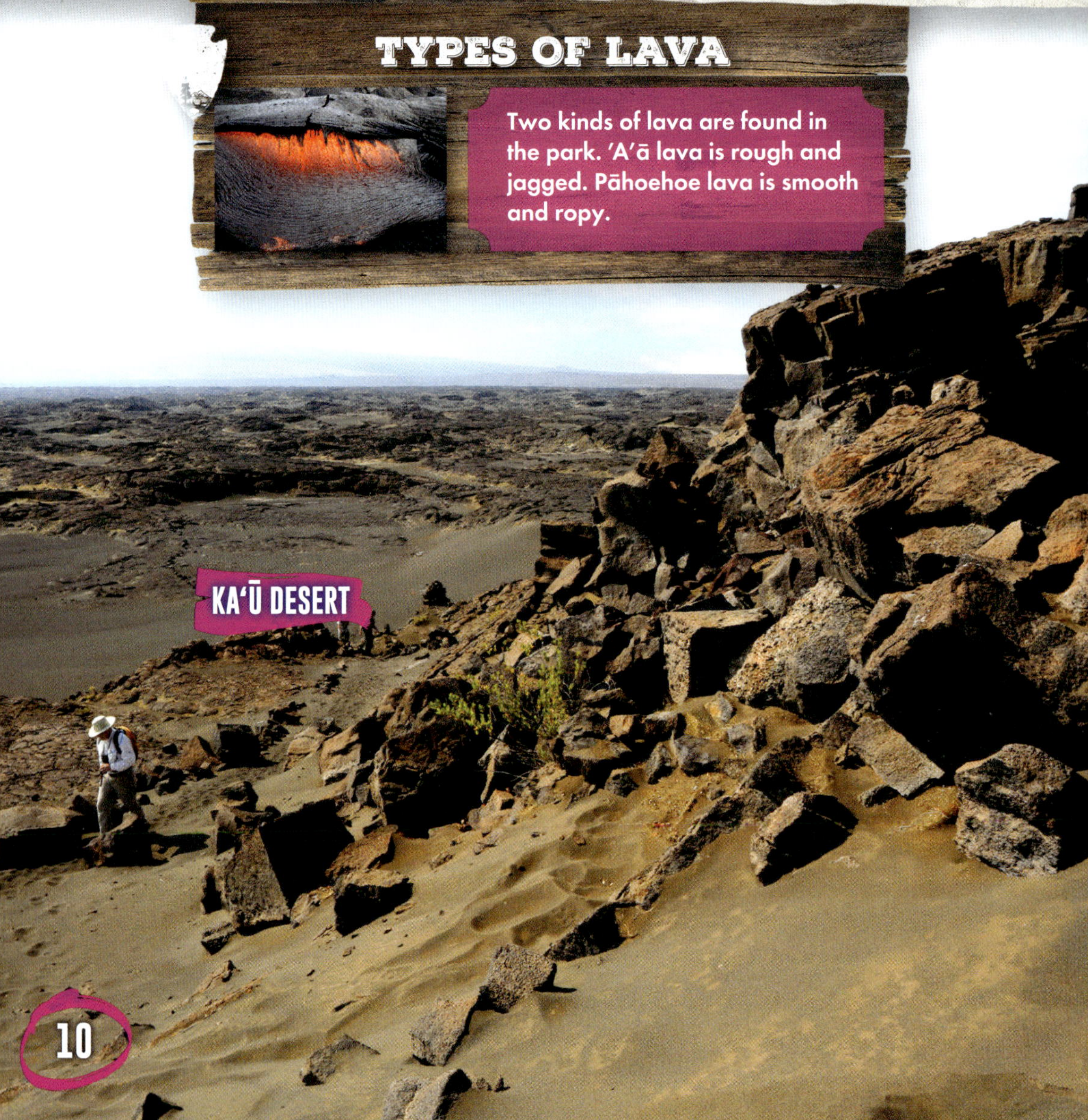

KA'Ū DESERT

Hawai'i Volcanoes is usually warm and moist at sea level. Temperatures are cooler in higher **elevations**. Snow can be found on the top of Mauna Loa. There, temperatures often fall below freezing at night.

PLANTS AND WILDLIFE

Hawai'i Volcanoes is home to many **native** plants and animals. Nēnē, the world's rarest geese, wander across lava fields on padded toes. 'Ae ferns grow nearby. Hawaiian hawksbill turtles, or honu'ea, swim in ocean waters. Hawaiian monk seals hunt for fish beneath the waves.

'Ōhi'a lehua trees are the park's most common tree. They grow throughout the park, even on lava! Hawaiian honeycreepers sip nectar from 'ōhi'a blossoms and eat insects off their leaves. Tiny Hawaiian hoary bats, or 'ōpe'ape'a, roost in 'ōhi'a branches. At sunset, they swoop through the air to hunt for moths.

'AE FERN

HAWAIIAN HAWKSBILL TURTLE

HAWAIIAN MONK SEAL

HAWAIIAN HONEYCREEPER

'ŌHI'A LEHUA

NĒNĒ

Life Span: about 12 years
Status: near threatened

The park's rainforest is packed with life. Kamehameha butterflies feed on the sap of koa trees. Hawai'i 'elepaio hunt insects on the bark. Yellow-faced bees buzz around uluhe ferns. Happy face spiders lay their eggs on kōpiko leaves.

Plants and animals live well in the harsh high elevations too. Mauna Loa silverswords grow between rocks on the volcano. Hawaiian petrels make nests in holes on Mauna Loa's high slopes. Wēkiu bugs eat insects blown in by the wind. Hawaiian hawks circle in the sky above.

MAUNA LOA SILVERSWORDS

HAWAIIAN HAWK

HUMANS IN HAWAI'I VOLCANOES NATIONAL PARK

LAVA CARVINGS

Early Hawaiians carved messages into solid lava. Around 23,000 of these carvings are found in a lava field in Pu'uloa in Hawai'i Volcanoes National Park. The earliest ones date back over 500 years.

LAVA CARVINGS

'ŌHI'A LEHUA TREE

Polynesians were the first people to live in Hawai'i. They arrived more than 1,000 years ago from distant islands. They traveled across the ocean in large canoes guided by the sun, stars, and seabirds.

The travelers brought pigs, dogs, and chickens. They carried seeds to grow taro, sweet potatoes, and bananas. They fished and collected salt along the shore. Gourds were used to collect rainwater. ʻŌhiʻa lehua trees were used to make houses and canoes. The people shared stories through chants and a dance called hula. For hundreds of years, the Hawaiian culture grew.

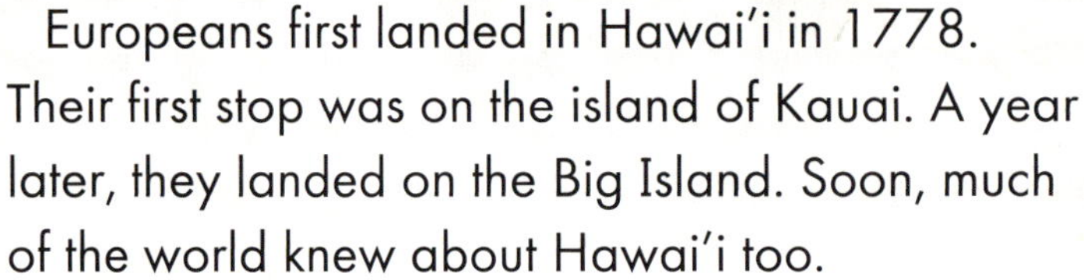

Europeans first landed in Hawai'i in 1778. Their first stop was on the island of Kauai. A year later, they landed on the Big Island. Soon, much of the world knew about Hawai'i too.

The Big Island began to see huge changes. In 1793, cattle were first brought to the island. **Plantations** rose up in the 1800s. News about the island's natural wonders attracted more outsiders. They brought in new ideas, non-native animals and plants, and diseases. The Hawaiian culture and land were changed forever.

MARK TWAIN

TWAIN'S TRAVELS

The author Mark Twain visited Kīlauea in 1866. His writings about the volcano made Hawai'i more popular.

COFFEE PLANTATION

HAWAIIAN VOLCANO OBSERVATORY IN 2010

In the early 1900s, scientists started coming to the Big Island to study volcanoes. The island's first volcano **observatory** was created by Thomas Jaggar in 1912. He continued to study the island's volcanoes for 28 years.

In 1916, President Woodrow Wilson created Hawai'i National Park to protect the volcanic landscape. It included parts of the Big Island and the island of Maui. In 1961, Hawai'i National Park was split into Haleakalā National Park on the island of Maui and Hawai'i Volcanoes National Park on the Big Island. Today, Hawai'i Volcanoes hosts more than one million visitors each year.

VISITING HAWAIʻI VOLCANOES NATIONAL PARK

Visitors from around the world come to see the park's volcanoes. They enjoy watching Kīlauea's activity from safe lookout points. Many hope to see it erupt! At night, people can sometimes watch glowing lava flows. Many people also come to see Hawaiian plants and wildlife. They learn about the deep connection between the volcanoes and the Hawaiian culture.

KĪLAUEA OVERLOOK

VOLCANO ART CENTER

People can view traditional Hawaiian art and watch hula performances at the Volcano Art Center inside the national park.

Hikers enjoy the park's many trails. They can discover volcanic wonders such as Pele's hair, which are thin glass threads made from lava. Those who seek a challenge can hike the Mauna Loa Trail to the top of the volcano!

PROTECTING THE PARK

Non-native plants and animals are among the park's greatest threats. Wild pigs destroy the forest floor. Mongooses, cats, and rats eat native birds and their eggs. Mosquitoes pass deadly diseases to native birds. Plants like strawberry guava and banana poka take over forests.

The volcanoes also pose dangers. They send gases, ash, and Pele's hair into the air. This makes breathing more difficult for people and wildlife. Lava flows can cover the land and destroy roads and buildings. **Climate change** decreases rainfall and increases the chance of wildfires. This creates threats for the land and wildlife.

STRAWBERRY GUAVA

HONEYCREEPER HIDEOUTS
Hawaiian honeycreepers mainly live in higher, cooler areas of the state. This helps them avoid mosquitoes living in lower areas that carry deadly bird diseases.
KĪLAUEA ERUPTION

People work hard to protect the park. Crews build fences to keep harmful animals out. They destroy unwanted plants to make space for native plants to grow. People track daily volcanic activity. They give warnings if they think volcanoes are going to erupt.

Visitors can also protect the park. They should stay on trails and clean their shoes before entering forests. This helps prevent harmful seeds and diseases from spreading. Visitors should not pick flowers, collect lava, or feed wildlife. They should remember the land is sacred to Hawaiian people. By working together, everyone can protect the park!

HAWAI'I VOLCANOES NATIONAL PARK FACTS

Area: 554 square miles (1,435 square kilometers)

Area Rank: 23RD largest park

Date Designated:
August 1, 1916
(as Hawai'i National Park)
September 22, 1961
(as Hawai'i Volcanoes National Park)

Annual Visitors:
1,433,593 visitors in 2024

Population Rank: 22ND most visited park in 2024

Highest Point: Mauna Loa; 13,681 feet (4,170 meters)

TIMELINE

MORE THAN 1,000 YEARS AGO

The first Polynesians arrive from Marquesas Island

JANUARY 1779

Captain James Cook lands on the Big Island

1912

Thomas Jaggar creates the Hawaiian Volcano Observatory

FOOD WEB

REEF TRIGGERFISH

1961

Hawai'i National Park is split into Haleakalā National Park in Maui and Hawai'i Volcanoes National Park on the Big Island

AUGUST 1, 1916

Hawai'i Volcanoes National Park is created and named Hawai'i National Park

GLOSSARY

climate change—a human-caused change in Earth's weather due to warming temperatures

craters—bowl-shaped openings in the earth

culture—the beliefs, arts, and ways of life in a place or society

dormant—inactive

dunes—hills made of sand or other fine, loose materials

elevations—heights above sea level

erupt—to suddenly let out steam, water, or other materials

hot spot—a place where hot magma from deep within Earth rises up to form a volcano; hot spots do not move.

lava tube—a cave formed from cooled lava; lava is melted rock from a volcano.

magma—flowing melted rock within the earth

native—related to plants and animals that are originally from the area

observatory—a building that is used for studying the sky, stars, volcanoes, or weather

plantations—large farms that grow coffee beans, cotton, rubber, or other crops; plantations are mainly found in warm climates.

sacred—relating to spiritual or religious practice

sea level—the average level of the surface of the ocean

traditional—related to customs, ideas, or beliefs handed down from one generation to the next

volcanoes—holes in the earth that erupt hot ash, gas, or melted rock called lava

TO LEARN MORE

AT THE LIBRARY

Klepeis, Alicia Z. *Hawaii.* Minneapolis, Minn.: Bellwether Media, 2022.

Payne, Stefanie. *The National Parks: Discover All 62 Parks of the United States.* New York, N.Y.: DK Publishing, 2020.

Van Rose, Susanna. *Volcano & Earthquake.* New York, N.Y.: DK Publishing, 2022.

ON THE WEB

FACTSURFER

Factsurfer.com gives you a safe, fun way to find more information.

1. Go to www.factsurfer.com.

2. Enter "Hawaii Volcanoes National Park" into the search box and click 🔍.

3. Select your book cover to see a list of related content.

INDEX

The images in this book are reproduced through the courtesy of: PeopleImages, front cover; clayton Harrison, p. 3; Alexander Demyanenko, p. 4 (Nāhuku); SMJoness, pp. 4-5; MNStudio, pp. 6-7, 22; Kevin, p. 8; Rufiyaa/ Wikipedia, p. 10 (lava); imageBROKER.com/ Alamy Stock Photo, pp. 10, 15 (mauna Loa silverswords); Bryan Lowry/ Alamy Stock Photo, p. 11; AGAMI Photo Agency/ Alamy Stock Photo, pp. 12 (hawaiian honeycreeper), 29 (hawaiian hawk); Forest and Kim Starr/ Wikipedia, p. 12 ('Ae Fern); Tetsuo Arada, p. 12 (hawaiian Hawksbill turtle); TobiasTJones, p. 12 (hawaiian Monk seal); Gerlach Photos, p. 12 ('ohi'a lehua); J Marshall - Tribaleye Images/ Alamy Stock Photo, p. 13 (hawaiian hoary bats); steheap, p. 13 (nēnē); Science History Images/ Alamy Stock Photo, p. 14; Image Source Limited/ Alamy Stock Photo, p. 15; NPS Photo/ Wikipedia, p. 16 (lava carvings); Cavan-Images, p. 16 ('ohi'a lehua tree); Kenneth Keifer, pp. 16-17; A.F. Bradley/ Wikipedia, p. 18; Dmitri Kotchetov, pp. 18-19; Jason O. Watson/ Alamy Stock Photo, p. 20; Harris & Ewing/ Wikipedia, p. 21 (President Woodrow Wilson); theartist312, p. 21; John Elk III/ Alamy Stock Photo, p. 22 (Kīlauea Overlook); Olga, p. 23 (Crater Rim Drive); fnendzig, p. 23 (Kīlauea, Mauna Loa); picturist, p. 23 (Nāhuku); ZHAO YOULI, p. 24; BlankNotion, pp. 24-25; Kyo46, p. 25; Rob Hainer, pp. 26-27; NPS Photo/ M.Watanabe/ NPS, p. 27; Captain Sir Edward Belcher RN/ Wikipedia, p. 28 (more than 1,000 years ago); National Maritime Museum/ Wikipedia, p. 28 (1779); Ken Lund/ Wikipedia, p. 28 (1912); LouieLea, p. 29 (1916); Lost_in_the_Midwest, p. 29 (1961); slowmotiongli, p. 29 (hawaiian monk seal); Rajh, p. 29 (hawaiian honeycreeper); norinori303, p. 29 ('ohi'a lehua); juancajuarez, p. 29 (reef triggerfish).